So, You're Bipolar; Now What?

Catch That Fox

Catherine Ehlers, MA., LPC
Kali Blazer, BSME
Melissa Armbruster, MA.,LLP

Eternity Day LLC

So, You're Bipolar. Now What?
Catch That Fox

Scripture taken from the HOLY BIBLE, NEW INTERNATIONAL VERSION®. Copyright © 1973, 1978, 1984 by International Bible Society. Used by permission of Zondervan Publishing House. All rights reserved.

This booklet contains advice and information regarding mental health. This information should be used to supplement rather than replace the advice of your doctor or another health care professional. If you know or suspect that you have a health problem, it is recommended that you contact your doctor. All efforts have been made to ensure the accuracy of the information contained in this booklet as of the date of publication.

ISBN 979-8-89114-015-8 (paperback)
ISBN 978-1-958434-93-2 (e)

Rev. 2023.08.04

MainSpring Books
5901 W. Century Blvd
Suite 750
Los Angeles, CA, US, 90045

www.mainspringbooks.com

Table of Contents

Overview

This book is about you. Each person takes a different path towards wellness. This workbook can help you look at your lifestyle choices, track your progress, recognize patterns and begin to put together a wellness plan that fits you and your family.

The goal of this book is to help you create a foundation for a wellness plan; one that focuses on prevention instead of crises management.

Bipolar disorder can be a frightening and devastating illness. The good news is that many people with bipolar disorder can achieve stability once they have a wellness plan that helps to prevent the symptoms that characterize the disorder.

A step-by-step wellness plan is something that you and your family learn to develop over time.

This book will provide you with some tools to help you feel more empowered, while dealing with bipolar disorder in your life.

Learn to identify the early warning symptoms of bipolar disorder, so that you can implement your wellness plan to minimize the mood swings and to ultimately eliminate going into a bipolar episode.

Learn to identify and map your mood triggers, so that you can better control them.

Knowing which symptoms affect your life can help you prepare for and better cope with them.

Becoming more educated on bipolar disorder will help you change patterns of behavior or emotions that contribute to your illness.

Family members and friends will learn how best to interact and help their loved one who suffers from bipolar disorder.

As a friend or family member, you will learn how important you are as a member of your loved one's health care team.

Welcome to all of you who have opened this book!

For some of you, being diagnosed with bipolar disorder is a relief because at least now there is an explanation for what you have been going through.

For others, it is a shock and you are still in disbelief. No matter who you are, you will have to begin your journey to stability in the same place—right here— learning about what bipolar disorder is.

This book was written for YOU, the bipolar beginner. We hope it will simplify the process of decision making about what to do after you are diagnosed. This book was written as a guide, not as an in-depth clinical manual about bipolar disorder.

Use it to refer back to as you move through different phases of coping with the disorder. Let it remind you that you do not struggle alone. Use it as a source of encouragement, that life can be better.

Catch That Fox!

We are going to use the analogy of fox hunting to help you to understand the relationship between the bipolar disorder and its symptoms. We use the fox to symbolize the disorder and the fox's footprints to represent the symptoms you may experience when you have bipolar disorder.

In successful fox hunting, the hunter is educated about his prey, and is equipped with everything he will need to accomplish his goal; catching the fox. As you become the hunter, searching out the many bipolar symptoms, you will learn to detect the difference between personality and bipolar symptoms. As you learn the personality of the bipolar person well, you will become quick to notice any subtle changes in their behavior. You will be like the hound, instantly aware of the fox. In order to avoid future bipolar episodes you need to notice the symptoms quickly to prevent them from intensifying.

Throughout this book we will introduce you to the tools you will need to "catch your fox". You can learn to identify bipolar symptoms and limit the impact that they can have over your life.

As you read through the book, each time you see footprints on the page, look for the symptoms of bipolar disorder. You are the hunter learning to catch the fox (the bipolar disorder).

Pendulum

**Extreme
High Pole
Mania**

**Extreme
Low Pole
Depression**

The further the pendulum swings towards the pole, the more intense the symptoms will be.

Inflated Self-esteem

Unrealistic beliefs

Decreased need for sleep

Rapid speech

Flight of ideas

Racing thoughts

Loss of Clarity

Memory goes

Creative thinking

Disjointed thinking

Excitability

Distractibility

Agitation

Restlessness

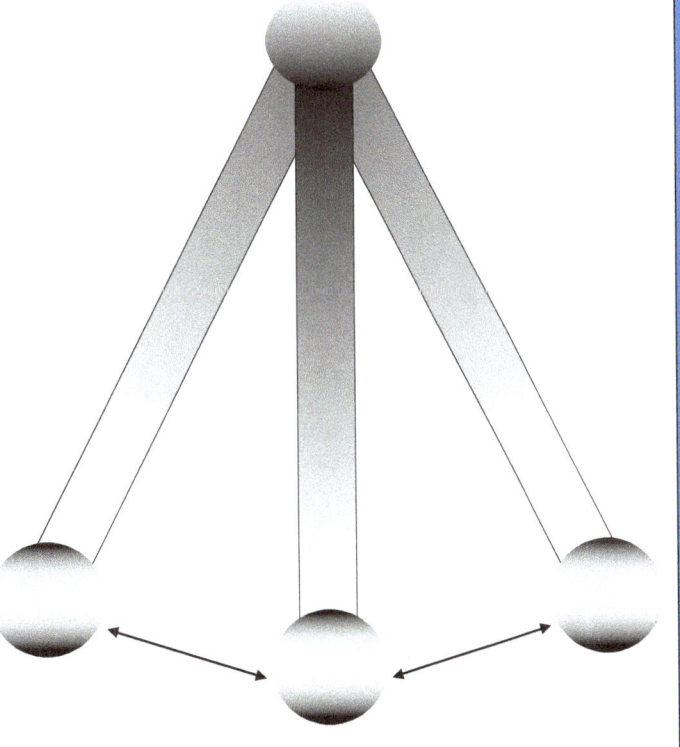

Lack of energy

Need extra sleep

No motivation

Weight loss/gain

Feel sad

Suicidal

Feel detached

Unable to make simple decisions

Trouble concentrating

Extreme fatigue

Despair

Feel guilty

Constant worry

Loose interest in everything

Bipolar Definition Symbolized by a Pendulum

Bipolar is a mood disorder caused by abnormalities in your brain chemistry that cause changes in your moods, energy and ability to function. The mood disorder is called bipolar, because your emotional state swings between two opposite poles of extreme highs and extreme lows.

The pendulum is a tool we use to give you a clearer picture of the variety of symptoms you may be experiencing. As you can see, the closer the pendulum swings to either pole, the more intense your symptoms will be.

The good news is that there are things you can do to prevent, reduce or minimize your mood swings and the symptoms they produce. We believe that with the proper medication, counseling, coping strategies and tools, you will be able to manage your bipolar more effectively.

Bipolar Disorder
An easier way to understand it

Having bipolar disorder is like living life on a roller coaster. Your life is filled with unpredictable ups and downs. However, unlike a roller coaster, the ride never ends.

As your mood swings toward manic, the ride to the top fills you with excitement and anticipation. When your mood reaches a manic peak, you feel fantastic! The incredible rush makes you feel like you're on top of the world. Your brief moment at the top comes to an end with a sudden downward plunge.

You feel yourself descending rapidly into a deep pit of darkness that is sucking the life out of you, yet you're powerless to stop it. Then with a crash, your roller coaster ride ends, and you find yourself at the bottom of the same horrible pit the roller coaster often leaves you in. You can feel the darkness permeating your body as those familiar, depressing thoughts and feelings begin to creep in to torment you to your core. Although there are a variety of places the roller coaster has left you, this depression pit is the worse because its visitors believe it's a place of no return! Over time and after numerous experiences on the roller coaster, you just try to find ways to survive the ride.

If this sounds like your life, or the life of your loved one, we want you to know that you can get off the roller coaster. It takes hard work and determination to manage your severe bipolar mood swings, but the results are worth the effort.

We hope this book helps you to finally get off the roller coaster ride; others have, and so can you.

Diagnosing Bipolar Disorder

Medical and Mental Health professionals use the <u>Diagnostic and Statistical Manual of Mental Disorders</u> or DSM as a guide in diagnosis. This manual provides clear descriptions and classifications of mental disorders to be used as a guideline in diagnosis by those with specialized clinical training, knowledge and skill in the mental health field.

In the DSM there are four major kinds of diagnoses for bipolar.

Bipolar I

Often referred to as "manic depressive". This type of bipolar is the easiest to diagnose because of the more obvious manic episode that is a necessary criteria for this diagnosis. It is often preceded or followed by a bout of depression and often severe enough to require hospitalization.

Bipolar II

This form of bipolar often appears more like a major depression with periodic periods of hypomania. The Hypomanic episodes can seem like "I am back to normal and I feel great" and often prolong accurate diagnosis. Many people with this type of bipolar experience anxiety as well, further delaying proper diagnosis. Necessary criteria is one Major Depressive episode followed by at least one Hypomanic episode.

Cyclothymic Disorder

The person with this type of bipolar experiences numerous periods of hypomanic symptoms and numerous periods of depressive symptoms that are not severe enough to be considered a "Major Depressive Episode". The swings between hypomania and depression can be constant and extremely stressful. The criteria for this diagnosis is at least two years of hypomanic symptoms and depression that is not considered a Major depressive episode.

Bipolar Disorder – Not Otherwise Specified (NOS)

This is a person with bipolar features that don't follow a particular pattern.

Note: Getting a diagnosis can allow you to receive the proper medical care and therapy that more effectively addresses your experience. A diagnosis can also legitimize your struggle and help you to begin taking the steps toward acceptance and stability.

Depressive Episode Symptoms

- Insomnia
- Mood and energy levels drastically shift
- Mood and energy very low or very high
- Fragile emotions
- Lack energy
- Stay in bed, need extra sleep
- Lack of basic motivation
- Weight gain or loss
- Feel sad or depressed, helpless or suicidal
- Feelings of detachment
- Feelings of guilt
- Feel a constant dread inside
- Constant worry – can't let worries go
- Inability to function well at work or socially
- Trouble concentrating; mind feels clouded or locked up
- Unable to make simple decisions
- Can't think of what to do
- Unable to cope with criticism or harsh words
- Feel isolated
- Loss of interest
- Extreme fatigue
- Body pains with no physical cause
- Have trouble sleeping - too much or too little
- Extreme anxiety, agitation, irritability
- Weighed down by everything
- Extremely sensitive
- Cry a lot
- Despair
- Deep, ongoing sadness
- Feeling numb
- No interest in personal hygiene
- Not wanting to do anything
- Just the thought of doing something feels like a heavy weight
- Feel useless, worthless, hopeless and a burden to everyone
- A desire to die to be freed from the agony of the depression
- Negative and pessimistic (why try, nothing helps)

Manic Episode Symptoms

- Inflated self-esteem or grandiosity (overestimate abilities and talents)
- Unrealistic beliefs in one's abilities and powers
- Decreased need for sleep without experiencing fatigue (e.g. feels rested after only 3 hours sleep)
- Rapid speech, more talkative than usual or pressure to keep talking
- Flight of ideas; jumping from one idea to another
- Overwhelming confusion replaces clarity
- Memory loss
- Creative thinking
- Disoriented and disjointed thinking
- Humor is extreme and inappropriate
- Your friends become frightened
- Objectivity decreases
- Excitability
- Distractibility
- Agitation or restlessness
- Increase in goal-oriented activities
- Increased sensitivity to sound and/or light

Hypomanic Episodes

Hypomanic episodes are very similar to manic episodes in that they share many of the same symptoms. The major difference is that *hypomanic* symptoms are not as extreme as manic symptoms are, so they're harder to identify.

When in a *hypomanic* episode, you feel great, you're very productive, and you need less sleep. One morning you wake up and all that energy is gone and you feel so exhausted, you can't get out of bed. It's the crash that identifies you just had a *hypomanic* episode. Sadly you realize your life has become a predictable pattern of gaining ground then losing the ground you gained. The following diagram shows *hypomanic* episodes of high energy and productive periods that end with a crash.

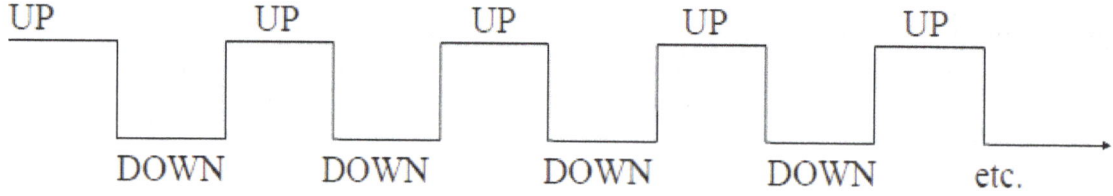

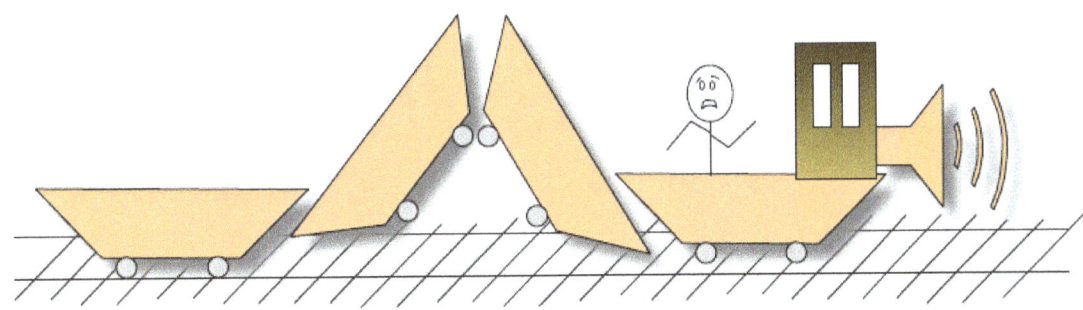

Bipolar Episode Description

Having an undiagnosed, untreated, un-medicated bipolar episode is like being hit by a train that you didn't see coming. It happens so fast that you didn't even know what happened.

To avoid future train wrecks you need to get the right medical attention for proper diagnosis, medication, and treatment, from a psychiatrist or your regular physician.

Knowing what your bipolar symptoms are and being able to recognize them early can help you avoid future bipolar episodes.

BIPOLAR LOCATION MAP

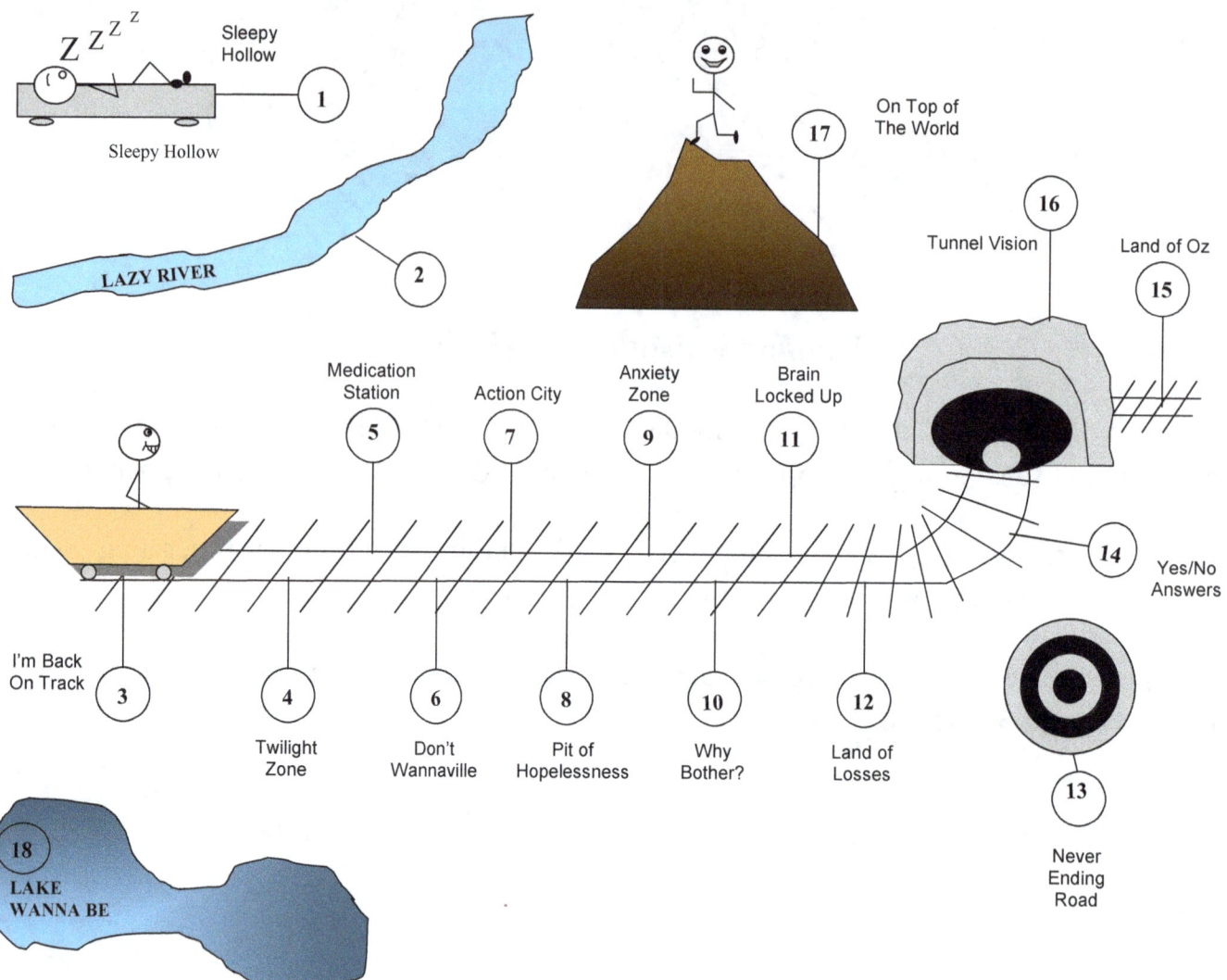

Bipolar Location Map Explanation

This map is a tool used to determine where you are in terms of your bipolar symptoms. The map symbolizes a train going along on tracks with different stops at stations along the way. These train stations represent a symptom or state of bipolar. You can use this tool to get a snap shot of where someone is relative to their bipolar symptoms. You can check off as many that apply at that given time. It is great for generating discussion on the topic of bipolar. Below are some train station example descriptions. There is no specific order. You can personalize them to be your own description.

1 - Sleepy Hollow

A place where you sleep all day and all night. You know you should get out of bed, but you just don't.

2 - Lazy River

You can get up, but you can't get going or stay going. Get up, but then go right back to bed.

3 - I'm Back on Track

Things are going good. You are back on a regular sleep schedule. You are back to your daily activities. You are accomplishing things. You are socializing. You feel confident. Medication is working to stabilize your symptoms.

4 - Twilight Zone

You feel sedated. You look overmedicated.

5 - Medication Station

The process of going through trial and error with different medications to find the one to help stabilize you. This can be a long and agonizing place because some medications take weeks to kick in. If the medication is not working, you have to slowly wean off the medication onto another. In the meantime, your symptoms may be getting worse. Even when your medication is working, you may experience unpleasant side effects.

6 - Don't Wannaville

You are out of bed, but don't want to do anything.

7 - *Action City*

A place of high productivity. Zipping through to-do lists. Staying up late getting things done and still getting up early. Taking on projects.

8 - *Pit of Hopelessness*

Deep darkness. Like a wet blanket of despair. You feel so close to the brink of hell that you can literally smell 'sulfur'. You may think about suicide as a way of escape.

9 - *Anxiety Zone*

This is where your thoughts can get fixated on a negative situation and lead to feelings of fretting, anxiety, guilt, and a feeling of being overwhelmed. Logically you know better, but knowing does not change it. The worry and anxiety has a mind of its own.

10 - *Why Bother?*

What is the point? Who cares?

11 - *Brain Locked Up*

You are aware of your surroundings, but you cannot respond. Someone asks you a personal question and your brain locks up. You know that the person is sitting there waiting for an answer, which makes it worse, but there is nothing on your radar screen.

12 - *Land of Losses*

Grieving over the loss of career, money, status, family, or friends.

13 - *Never Ending Road*

Mood swings are occurring more frequently; it seems like they will never end.

14 - *Yes/No Answers*

You can't deal with open ended questions or simple questions like "do you want your sandwich on bread or toast?" You just need the other person to decide.

15 - *Land of Oz*

Loss of objectivity. Your perception does not match with reality.

16 - *Tunnel Vision*

You seem to have only one way of viewing a situation or one feeling about an event. It is usually negative even when logic would dictate otherwise.

17 - *On Top of the World*

You are so high on life you can hardly stand it. It is like training for a marathon or a 230 mile bike ride. You actually believe that you have made it and will never have to taste the pit of depression again. You believe you are off the roller coaster forever.

18 - *Lake Wanna Be*

You want to be back to your old self. You want to get back everything you have lost. You want to get back to normal.

Recognizing Bipolar Mood Swings

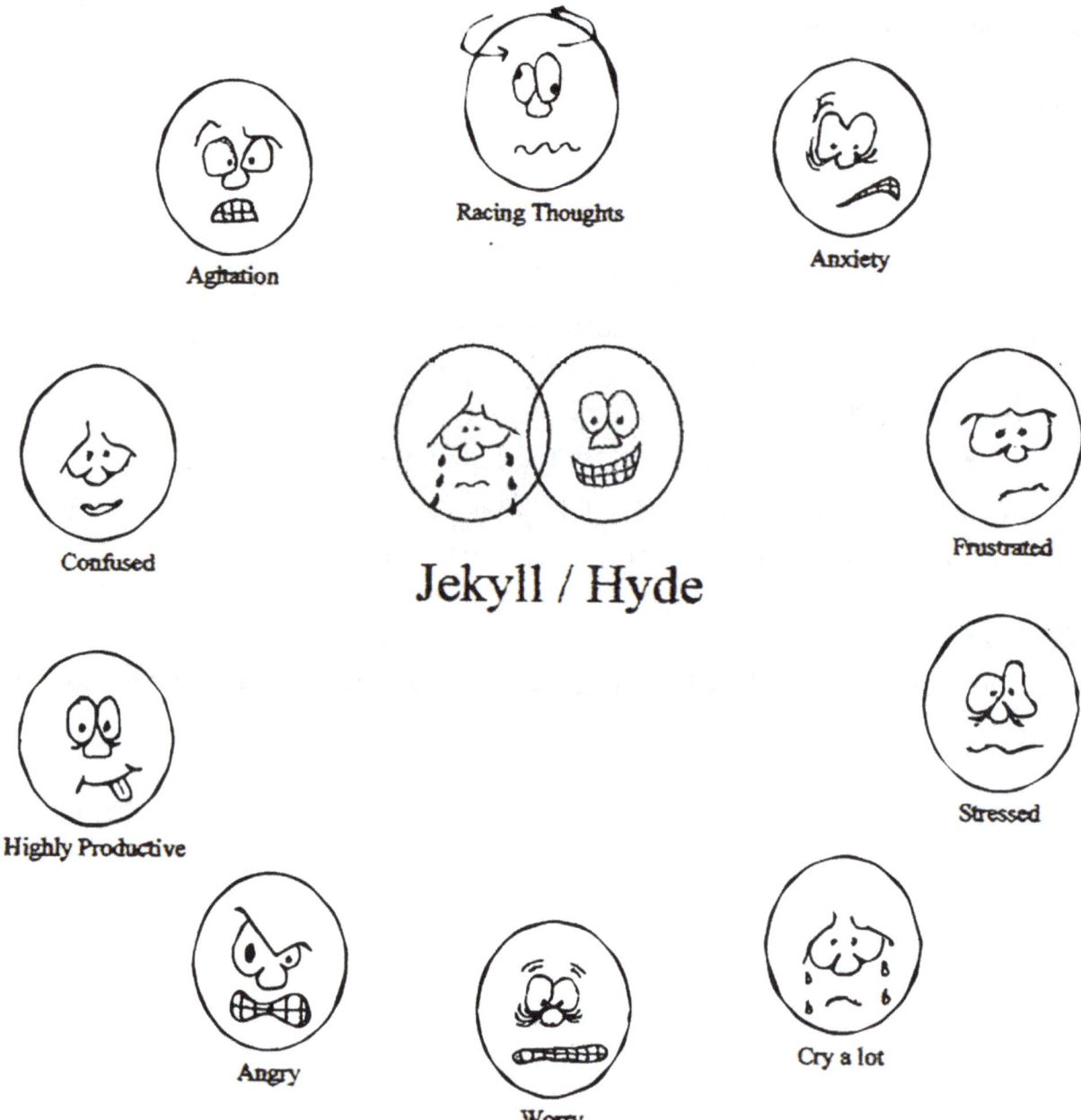

A Bipolar Depression Episode Is like being in a Train Wreck In the Land of OZ

A Bipolar Depressive Episode Is Like Being In A Train Wreck

- You feel…………….Broken.
- You want…………..The depression to end.
- You think…………..You will be like this forever.
- You believe………....Because you can't make yourself do anything, you have no value.
- You fear…………….You'll never get 'you' back.
- Your pain…………...Losing your identity, job, respect, value, control and the old you.
- You're convinced….That you're a disappointment to yourself and others.

Going through a Depressive Episode is like living in the Land of Oz.

- Everything about you changes.
- Your reality is distorted.
- Your objectivity disappears.
- Your independence is greatly reduced.
- You can't think clearly.
- You feel confused.
- Your eating changes.
- Your hopes, dreams and goals come to a screeching halt.
- You feel alone and of little value.
- You lose everything.
- Your joy is turned into sorrow.
- You feel awful; mentally, physically and psychologically.
- You need and want help.
- You can't get out of bed.

The Bipolar Depression Pit

When people experience a bipolar depression, they say it feels like they're in a deep, dark pit that they can't get out of. They describe their depression as a darkness that is so dark, it reaches their soul. They become deeply troubled, distressed and exceedingly sorrowful to the point of death. Their soul feels so downcast; they lose the desire to live.

Jesus describes His experience with those same feelings, prior to going to the cross. He says in Mark 14:32 that He was troubled and deeply distressed and that His soul was exceedingly sorrowful – even to death. What did He do about those feelings? He fell on the ground and prayed to His Father and asked His disciples for prayer support.

God knows when you are in the pit because He promises He will never leave you! He promises you in Psalm 23, that when you go through the valley of the shadow of death, He'll be in that valley with you. He will send you help to get you through and comfort you while you're in it; He does not sit idly by. Like Jesus in the garden, we want God to remove this 'cup' from us; knowing all things are possible for Him; yet His will may be to walk through it with us. When you are in this valley of death, look for the lilies in the valley. The lilies will be there to remind you He truly is with you every step of the way.

If God can and did raise Christ from the dead, and promises to raise us up from the dead, then surely He can raise you up from the pit of darkness – if you'll let Him. Call upon the Lord in your day of distress and He will answer you. Make Him your refuge in time of trouble. He hears your cries and sees your tears. In fact, He says He records every tear you shed in His book and saves them in a bottle. When you get to heaven and ask Him: Didn't you notice me in those dark and awful pits? Did I matter to you, did you care? He will then show you how much your tears mattered to him because He will open the book and show every tear you ever cried was recorded in His book about you and every tear you've shed has been saved in a bottle (Ps 56:8). Yes, you do matter a lot to Him. He may even say that on earth, we love our children so much we save their first tooth when it falls out, or their first pair of booties, but He saves our tears, as evidence that not one went unnoticed. He will also point out the lilies He placed in our valley to comfort and help us through it. He may even mention the names of the people who helped you during that time and then ask you: "didn't you recognize Me???"

Yes, you are a sheep under His care (Psalm 95:7). Wouldn't He notice if one of His sheep fell into a deep, dark pit? Would He sit idly by and do nothing? Of course not! Like any 'good'

Shepard, He would go to work immediately to pull it out. He says you are much more valuable to Him than a sheep (Luke 12:11). Reach out your hand for help and you will feel someone grasp it to help raise you up and out. I hope you recognize "Him."

<u>Bible Verses:</u>

Psalm 139

Psalm 55:4-7

Psalm 18:28

Psalm 116

Psalm 119:173

Psalm 121:1-2

Psalm 138:7

Psalm 61:3-4

Steps of Hope

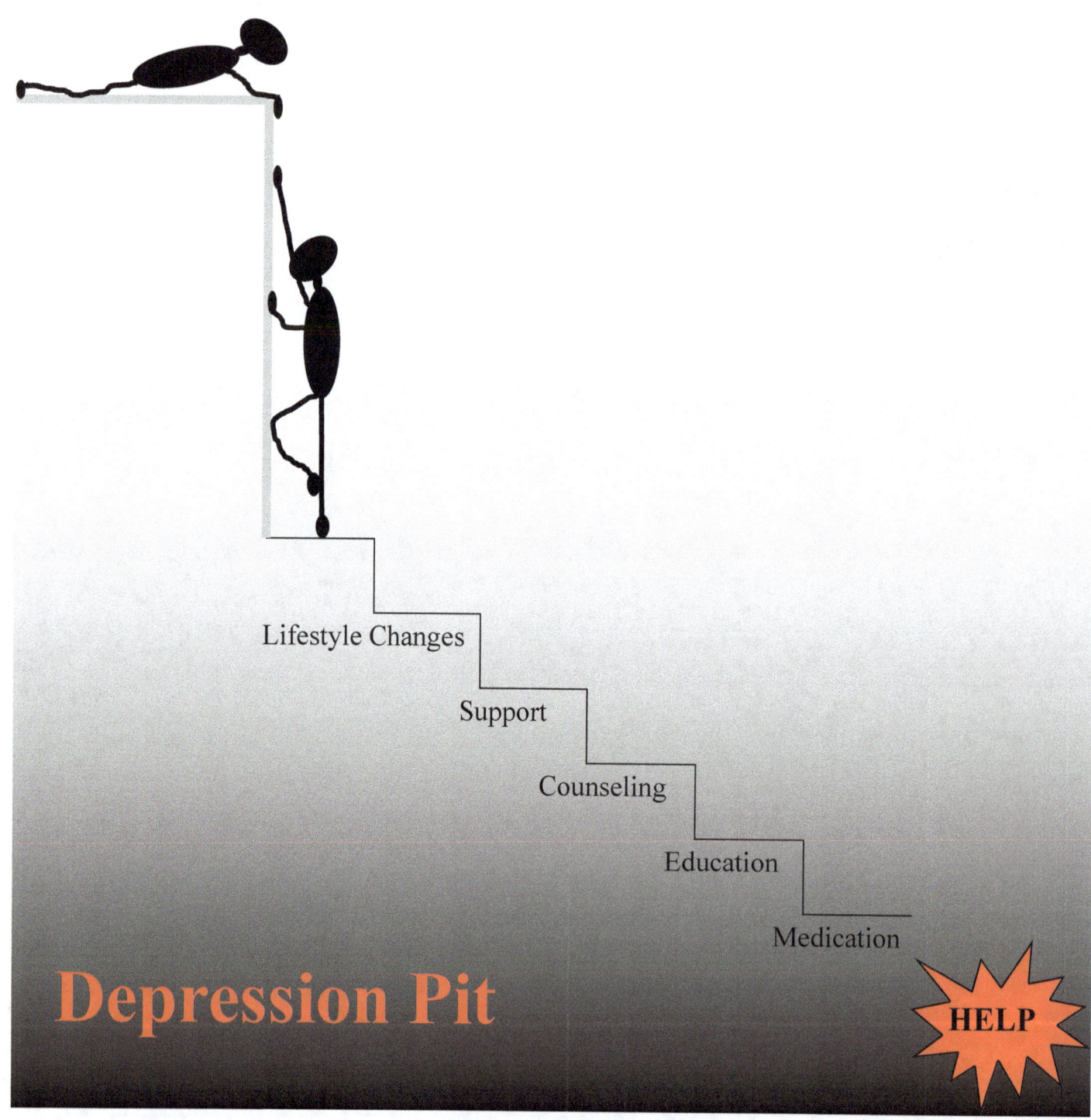

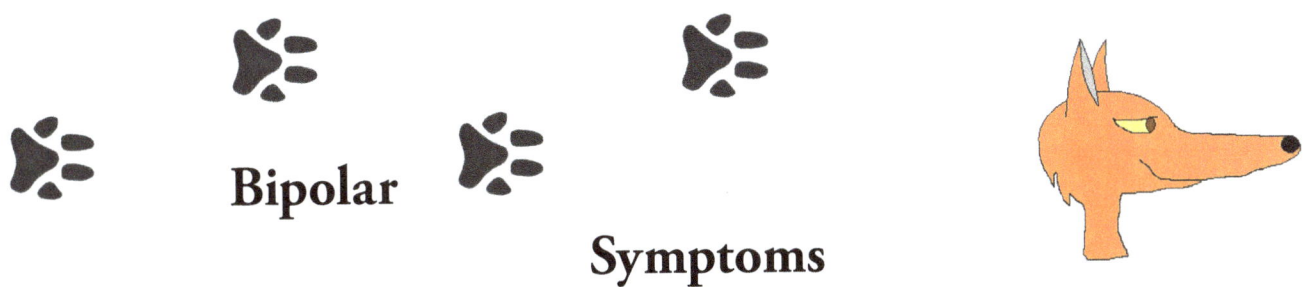

Bipolar

Symptoms

<u>Our Ultimate Goal is to stabilize our moods by managing our bipolar.</u>

<u>We use many tools to reach our goal.</u>

Tools are what we use to stabilize our mood swings, avoid or minimize episodes, and reduce the effects bipolar symptoms have on our lives. The following questions are a tool to help move you closer to the goal of managing your bipolar. The more questions you answer yes to, the closer you are to attaining your goal.

- Have you been diagnosed by a doctor?
- Do you know what bipolar is?
- Are you educated on bipolar?
- Is your spouse, family or close friend educated on it?
- Are you educated on bipolar medication?
- Are you aware of the seriousness of the disorder?
- Are you aware that bipolar can be better managed with medication, hard work, determination and the right tools?
- Are you on medication right now?
- Is your medication working; meaning has it stabilized your mood and episodes?
- Have you had counseling for your bipolar?
- Have you attended bipolar groups or workshops?
- Have you read books on bipolar?
- Do you have a good support system or at least a support person?
- Are you and your support person willing to learn how to manage your bipolar?
- Are you aware that with medication and the right tools, you can learn to manage bipolar, but it is a long process?
- Do you know what a bipolar conversation is?
- Do you know what's helpful and what isn't?
- Is your job enjoyable or stressful?
- Is your home a place of refuge or is it stressful?
- How do you see life in regards to living with bipolar?
- Do you have hope?

Catch that Fox!

RECOVERY

Emotional healing takes place in a safe, supportive environment. Developing a dependable support system will be important to successfully managing your bipolar.

Support System Tools

1. A Therapist Who:
- Is educated about bipolar disorder.
- Is non-judgmental.
- Is encouraging.
- Helps with personal responsibility and accountability.
- Is willing to work with your doctor in managing your symptoms and medication.
- Provides a safe environment for recovery.

2. A Doctor or Psychiatrist Who:
- Is accessible.
- Makes you feel comfortable.
- Answers your questions.
- Has expertise on bipolar disorder.

3. A Dependable Support Person(s) Who:

- Instills hope.
- Encourages you.
- Strengthens you.
- Constantly assures you that you will get through this; it won't go on forever.
- Is happy to help you.
- Is willing to stay with you.
- Assures you they won't leave you.
- Will do what it takes to help you get through this.
- Says encouraging words.
- Does for you what you can't do for yourself.
- Uses no condemnation or harsh words.
- They make you feel safe and loved.
- Will stick with you, no matter how long that takes.

Bipolar Support System

Some may ask; what about me? It would be great if I had this kind of support, but I don't. What do people like me do, who have no one to help them?

God invites everyone to look to Him for all our needs, because He is able to help us. The Bible is full of stories of people who faced serious difficulties and had to depend on God to supply all their needs.

God's Word assures us that He has not left us as orphans to fend for ourselves. In fact, He says that we are 'never' alone, because He will never leave us and nothing can separate us from His love.

Whenever you feel you have no one to help you, remember God knows what you're up against and offers His help. He invites you to come boldly to the Throne of our gracious God. There we will receive mercy, and we will find grace to help us when we need it. (Hebrews 4:16, New Living Bible).

The verses listed below are to encourage you to put your trust in God, because He loves you deeply and unconditionally.

Verses: Psalm 139 (Very good)

II Corinthians 1:3-4 *Praise be to the God and Father of our Lord Jesus Christ, the Father of compassion and the God of all comfort, who comforts us in all our troubles, so that we can comfort those in any trouble with the comfort we ourselves have received from God.* (NIV)

Psalm 40:1 *I waited patiently for the Lord; He turned to me and heard my cry. He lifted me out of the slimy pit, out of the mud and mire; He set my feet on a rock and gave me a firm place to stand.* (NIV)

Psalm 69:14-18 *Rescue me from the mire, do not let me sink; deliver me from those who hate me, from the deep waters. Do not let the floodwaters engulf me or the depths swallow me up or the pit close its mouth over me. Answer me, O Lord, out of the goodness of Your love, in Your great mercy turn to me. Do not hide Your face from Your servant; answer me quickly, for I am in trouble. Come near and rescue me.* (NIV)

Bipolar Triggers

Education is the most helpful tool for preventing bipolar episodes. Mood swings are often caused by chaos, stress and lack of sleep. It's important to know what your emotional triggers are. Everyone is different, what triggers one person won't necessarily trigger someone else. Learn what your emotional triggers are and create an action plan to respond to them. Following is a list of the most common bipolar triggers:

- Stress!!!
- Arguments
- Chaos
- Stressful family and personal relationships
- Too many commitments or responsibilities
- Poor sleeping habits
- Stressful world events
- Illness or death of loved one
- Drugs and alcohol use
- Poor diet
- Lack of exercise
- A stressful job
- A move or major change
- Lack of balance, structure or schedule
- Negative internal self-talk
- Driving in traffic
- Feeling unheard or not understood by friends and/or family

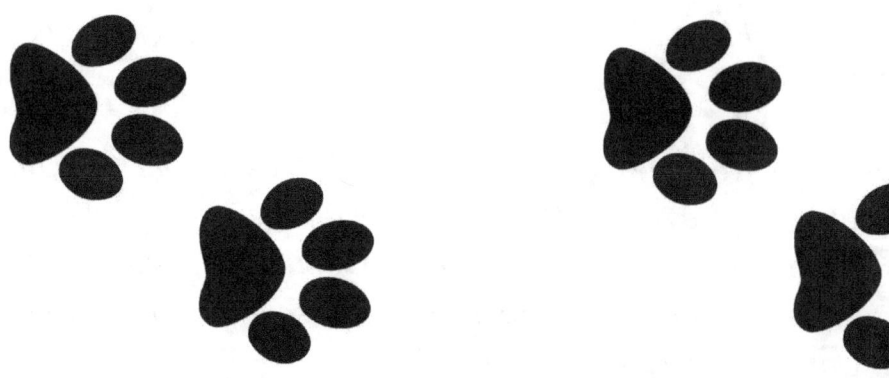

LEARN TO RECOGNIZE AND DESCRIBE YOUR OWN SYMPTOMS FOR DEPRESSION, STRESS, ETC., BY USING THIS TEMPLATE.

THE FOLLOWING IS AN EXAMPLE OF THE SYMPTOM OF STRESS.

1. <u>What does it feel like when you are stressed?</u>

Agitation, irritability, too much energy inside my "skin", internal storm, confusion, can't keep my mind on one thing, nervousness, fear (but don't know what is frightening me), worry, tension, can't sleep, everything seems unbearable, keyed up, restlessness, frustrated, self-criticism, guilt, cycle of fluctuating moods, and constantly changing feelings.

2. <u>How does it show?</u>

Unproductive, can't accomplish anything, can't focus, can't relax and get comfortable sitting, foot bounces, pacing, picking at nails, can't sit still, loss of appetite, can't fall asleep, difficult staying asleep, always having to take a deep breath (like I am not getting enough air in just regular breathing), depression dip, risky behavior, and high energy.

3. <u>What thoughts run through your mind?</u>

I can't deal with this, this is too much to handle, I spin the situation over and over and over, I can't think, I can't focus, I know my spinning mind is wrong, yet I can not stop it from spinning, it seems hopeless. Constantly changing thoughts, contemplating suicide. I think that I have no control of the situation.

4. <u>What do you do?</u>

Talk about it to a friend, go to scripture, avoidance, try to focus on something else to take my mind off the situation, try to take the path of least resistance to solve the problem, worry, take medication, alcohol, sleep, exercise. Use Cognitive Behavior Therapy (CBT) techniques. Try to get rid of what's causing the stress (if possible), change my attitude toward what is causing the stress (hard to do), face up to what's causing the stress until it isn't stressful any more, try to do something I enjoy, express my emotions (crying relieves stress), work at creating a stress-free place in my home, talk to family or a friend, seek outside help when I simply can not handle the stress.

5. <u>How does it affect others?</u>

Stress can cause tension between me and others. It takes time and energy away from the other person and they worry over you.

6. <u>How do their reactions affect you?</u>

I sometimes feel bad and inadequate, because I think I should be able to handle the situation better than I am. Sometimes I feel better because it helps me clarify my thoughts and clarify the situation, and that helps me see solutions and options.

The Forest and The Tree -
A Bipolar Conversation

The popular phrase, 'You can't see the forest for the trees'; is a good way to describe bipolar. When someone is experiencing a bipolar episode, they lose the ability to see the bigger picture; all they see is the tree. Therefore, when they come out of their episodes, they are unable to understand what others are so upset about. Those of us that can see the forest, see the impact of their behavior, thinking and choices have had on everyone around them. They, on the other hand, see only the tree, and are unable to comprehend anything beyond it. Knowing and accepting the fact that they were not and are not aware of the bigger picture can decrease the pain and ineffective arguing that occurs after a bipolar episode.

Reality and objectivity is another difficult bipolar struggle; especially for those with mania that is only hypomania. Hypomanic symptoms often manifest as being highly motivated and productive. They feel good, look good, and appear to be back on track. Sometimes the only way you can tell that their sense of well being was a hypomanic episode is by the crash that immediately follows it. One day they wake up and they can't get out of bed, their motivation and well-being is replaced with exhaustion and depressed mood. This continues until they wake up one morning and for some reason, they feel good again. Unfortunately, during this down time, they have lost all the ground they gained during their hypomania phase. Immediately after a mood swing, they find themselves in a forest/tree bipolar argument. They're told about all the stress, pain and burden their time out placed on everyone else. Since they are unable to recall anything outside of the tree, they just end up arguing against others' reality.

Over time and after numerous arguments following on-going mood swings, they begin to lose their ability to enjoy even the good times. When they begin to feel a sense of well-being, along with positive and close friendships, they wonder if it's a hypomanic episode with disappointment waiting in the wings. They begin to question if the relationships are as close as they think they are, if their reality is again distorted. They have learned from previous episodes that things aren't often what they appear to be. The realization that they lack objectivity and are unable to trust their reality decreases their sense of stability and safety.

Stability comes with enlisting and accepting the help of others. Allow your support system to be your objectivity while you're learning how to manage your bipolar on your own. Bipolar symptoms can be managed and you can regain stability and objectivity, by learning your unique symptoms and how to avoid experiencing the extreme exhaustion and condemnation after a manic episode.

"LIFE IS A __GIFT__ FROM GOD AND YOU MUST LIVE IT"

A bipolar survivor who caught that fox

Epilogue

God says that "all things God works for good" and "He can give us beauty for ashes." Romans 8:28 and Isaiah 61:3.

In other words – your suffering (ashes) are worth gold in God's hands and kingdom. In fact, this booklet was made from the ashes of those who have made the journey of recovery. Their hearts are here in every word and picture placed in this booklet.

You are surrounded by a cloud of survivors, who are encouraging you on.

May you find the lilies in your valleys and the gold in your ashes and join the cloud of survivors encouraging those who will be traveling the same journey you have.

CONCLUSION

NOW YOU HAVE LEARNED THE BASICS ABOUT BIPOLAR DISORDER AND HAVE HAD A CHANCE TO HEAR FROM OTHERS WHOSE LIVES HAVE BEEN IMPACTED BY IT. YOU NOW HAVE SOME CHOICES TO MAKE FOR YOURSELF. BORROWING A PHRASE FROM THE POPULAR TWELVE STEP PROGRAMS, WE HOPE YOU DO THE 'NEXT RIGHT THING' FOR YOURSELF AND YOUR LOVED ONES. STAYING FOCUSED ON WHAT WASN'T RIGHT OR FAIR IN THE PAST WON'T CHANGE WHAT COULD BE RIGHT ABOUT TODAY OR TOMORROW. JOIN US IN CHOOSING TO LIVE LIFE MORE ABUNDANTLY AND CATCH THAT FOX!

References and Resources
from Reliable Sources

I. General information about Bipolar Disorder and Assistance:
1. National Suicide Prevention Lifeline:
Trained crisis workers are available to talk 24 hours a day, 7 days a week.
- *Call:* 1-800-273-8255
- *Chat online:* http://chat.suicidepreventionlifeline.org/GetHelp/ LifelineChat.aspx

2. The National Alliance for Mental Illness (NAMI):
Provides locally-based support and education about mental illness; a particularly good resource for families affected by a loved one's bipolar disorder.
- *Call: 1-800-950-6264*
- *Online:* www.nami.org
- Enter your state name to find a list of the affiliates in cities throughout the state.
  i. NAMI in Michigan: http://www.namimi.org#sthash.SFrgongr.dpuf

---

II. General Information about Bipolar Disorder – Reliable Sources Updated Regularly
1. National Institute of Mental Health:
https://www.nimh.nih.gov/health/topics/bipolar-disorder/index.shtml

2. US Department of Health and Human Services (HHS):
Evidence-based information about bipolar, updated information regarding bipolar research. Enter zip code to find providers.
- *Online:* www.mentalhealth.gov

3. Depression and Bipolar Support Alliance:
General information about bipolar, wellness strategies, linkage to support.
- *Online:* http://www.dbsalliance.org/

III. Bipolar Research Published in Peer-reviewed Academic and Medical Journals

1. United States, National Library of Medicine (National Institute of Health):
The World's Largest Medical Library.
- *Online:* https://www.nlm.nih.gov/

2. Medscape:
Medically-oriented access to numerous journals.
- *Online:* http://search.medscape.com/search/

3. American Psychiatry Association (APA):
General information for the public regarding bipolar disorder and support.
- https://www.psychiatry.org

4. APA Medical Journals:
Rigorous, medically-oriented journals; access may be limited.
- **APA Psychiatry Online:** http://psychiatryonline.org/
- **APA Psychiatric News:** http://psychnews.psychiatryonline.org/
- **APA American Journal of Psychiatry:** http://ajp.psychiatryonline.org/

5. APA Diagnostic and Statistical Manual of Mental Disorders (DSM):
The DSM serves as a universal authority for psychiatric diagnoses. Treatment recommendations, as well as payment by health care providers, are often determined by DSM classifications.
- ***Full text available online:*** http://dsm.psychiatryonline.org/doi/book/ 10.1176/appi. books.9780890425596

6. Psychcentral:
General information. Enter zip code to find providers in your area:
- https://psychcentral.com/disorders/bipolar/

IV: Medications Used to Treat Bipolar:

1. Drugs.com:
Fantastic resource for all medications, including those to treat bipolar. Search by medication name to find general information, interactions, side effects, Q&A.